Funny People

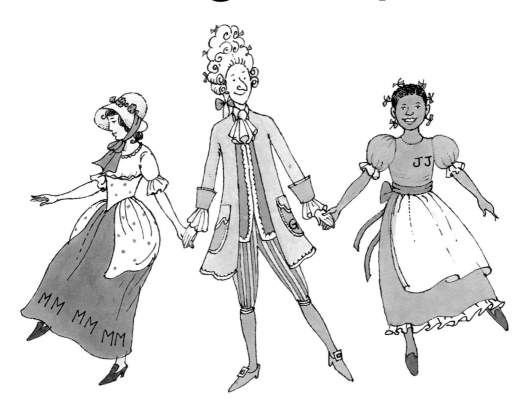

Written by Hilary Minns
Illustrated by Clyde Pearson

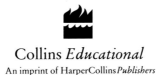

Collins *Educational*
An imprint of HarperCollins*Publishers*

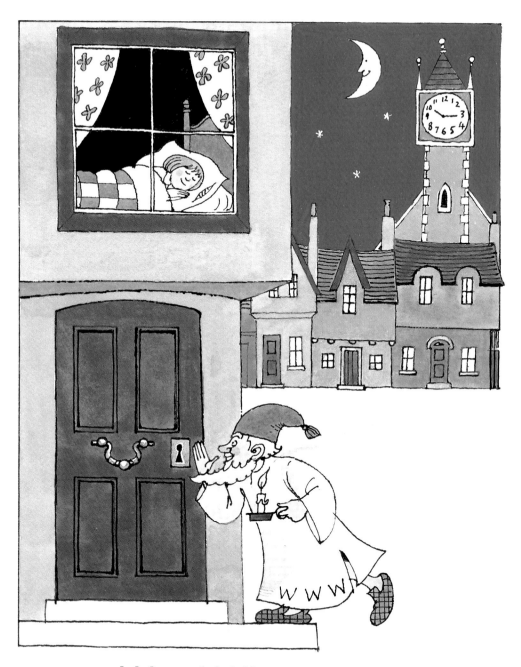

Wee Willie Winkie

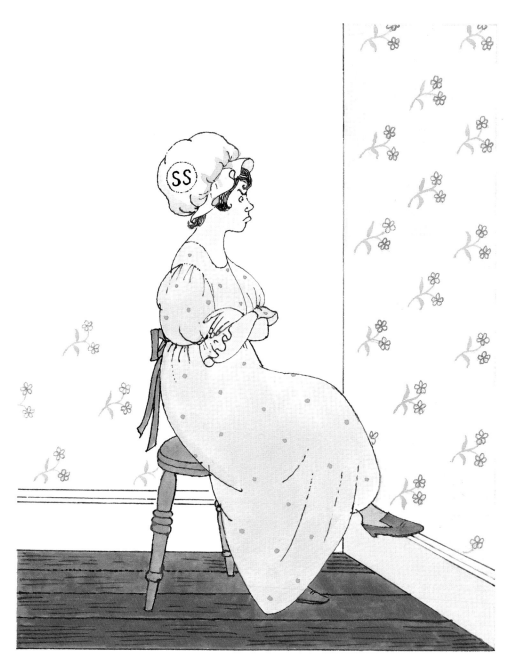

Sulky Sue

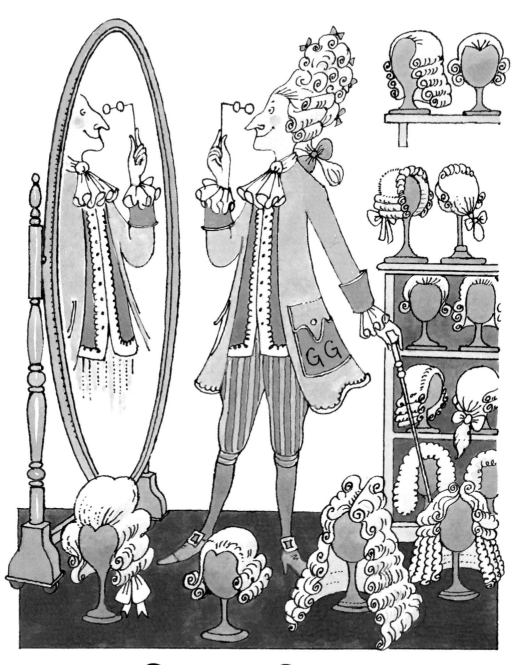

Gregory Griggs

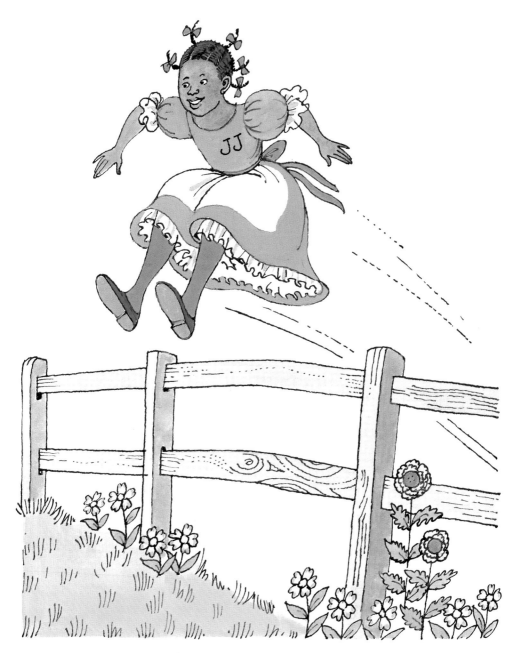

Jumping Joan

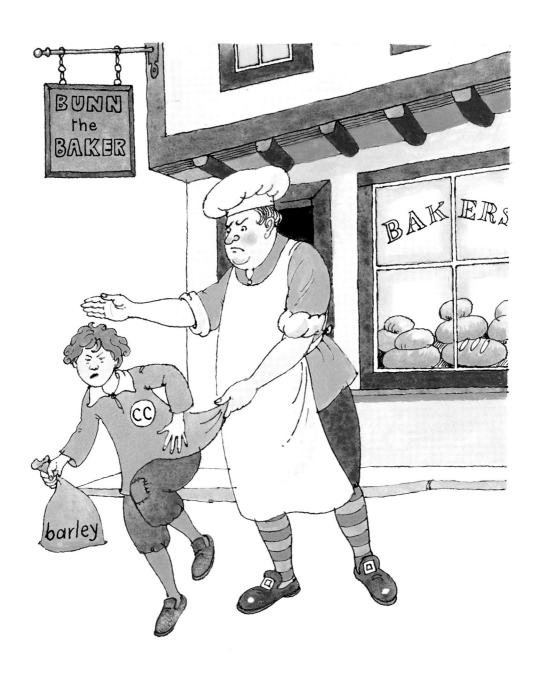

Charley, Charley

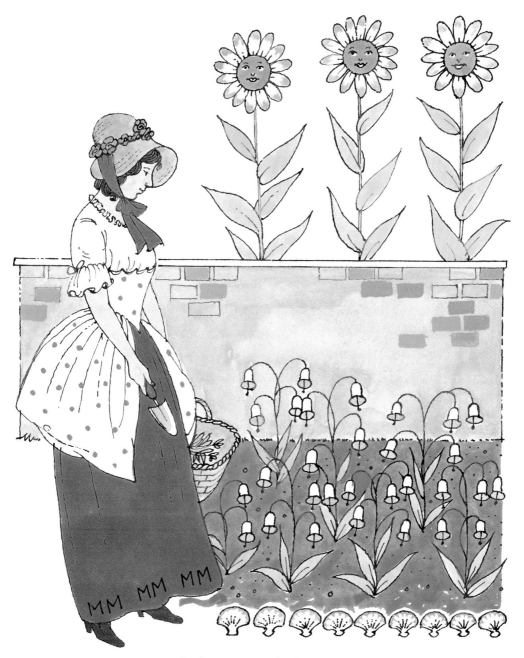

Mary, Mary

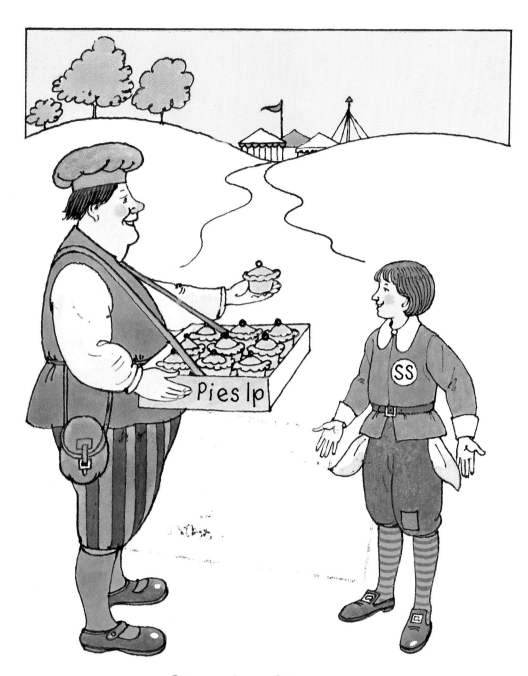

Simple Simon